Kids can Cook

D1364005

hinkler

With special thanks to Elena, Austin, Maya,
Lucy, Monique, Gerri and Rasa.

hinkler

Published by Hinkler Books Pty Ltd
45–55 Fairchild Street
Heatherton Victoria 3202 Australia
www.hinkler.com.au

Recipes and hero photos © R&R Publications 2011
Design and step-by-step photos © Hinkler Books Pty Ltd 2011

Cover images © Shutterstock.com: Red tomato isolated © Wolfe Larry/
shutterstock; Wooden spoon © Stephen Aaron Rees/shutterstock; One fettuccine
pasta nest isolated on white © Fribus Ekaterina/shutterstock; Olive oil, eggs,
spices and a wooden spoon on a white background © Aprilphoto/shutterstock.

Cover and Text Design: Sam Grimmer
Prepress: Graphic Print Group
Typesetting: R&R Publications
Photography: R&R Photostudio (www.rrphotostudio.com.au)
Recipe Development: R&R Test Kitchen

ISBN: 978 1 7418 4014 8

Printed and bound in China

contents

Cooking is Fun!

Learning to cook can be easy and fun, and a great skill to have when you're growing up. Preparing food helps to teach you about healthy eating, balanced meals and tasty ingredients, and means that you can look after yourself properly all the way through life.

Take some time to look through the recipes and see which ones you want to cook first. It doesn't matter whether you choose a recipe from the beginning or end of the book: each recipe is explained in simple terms with lots of pictures to show you what to do. In no time at all, you will be the best chef in your house!

What are you waiting for? Start cooking!

Weights and Measurements

Many recipe books use either metric measurements (g, kg, ml, l) or imperial measurements (oz, lb, fl oz) but this book makes things even easier by also using cups and spoons.

Remember:
- Learn your spoon sizes: teaspoon (smallest) and tablespoon (biggest) are the most commonly used in this book
- Use a measuring jug for liquids
- Packaged items such as meat show the weight on the packaging, usually in grams (g) or pounds (lb)

Stay Safe

Before you start to cook, read through the recipe instructions. Gather together all your ingredients. Then, look for the icon next to the photos. This means that you might need to ask an adult for help for that step; it could be to use a sharp knife, cook with the stove or oven, or use electrical equipment.

- Ask an adult to help you with cutting and to show you how to use a knife properly
- Always use a dry oven mitt to move items in and out of the oven
- Place hot dishes on a protected surface and DO NOT touch the dish with your bare hands

Clean Cooking

A good chef works in a clean kitchen, so start practising good habits today! Make sure your cooking area is clean before you start, and ALWAYS leave it clean and tidy when you have finished. That includes doing the washing up!

- Wash your hands before you start to cook
- Wear an apron to protect your clothes
- Run a bowl of hot, soapy water, and place dirty items in it as you cook; without soaking, raw ingredients go dry and crusty and are really hard to wash off
- Use separate utensils and chopping boards for raw meat
- If you use raw meat or raw eggs, wash your hands and wipe your surfaces immediately afterward

How to Use This Book

Ingredients List
Make sure you have all the food items that you need.

Adult Supervision Symbol
Check with an adult before you do this step.

Equipment List
Gather your tools before you start cooking.

Serving Information
Check how many serves the recipe makes, and how long it will take to prepare and cook. Nutritional details show how much energy and fat this food contains.

Notes
These boxes contain handy cooking hints and ideas for alternative ingredients.

crunchy granola

Makes
10 portions

Preparation
10 mins

Cooking
20 mins

Kilojoules/Calories
2058/490

Fat
22g/0.77oz

What do you get if you mix nuts, seeds, dried fruits, oats, and lovely, sticky honey and syrup? You get the healthiest, most delicious breakfast imaginable, that's what!

Ingredients

½ cup honey

½ cup natural maple syrup

4 cups rolled oats

1 cup almonds, roughly chopped

½ cup walnuts, roughly chopped

½ cup sunflower seeds

½ cup pumpkin seeds

1 cup dried apricots, sultanas (golden raisins), cranberries (craisins) and apple

1 teaspoon ground cinnamon

1 Preheat the oven to 180°C (350°F). Warm the honey and the maple syrup in a small saucepan.

2 Combine all of the remaining ingredients in a large bowl.

Equipment

3 Add the warmed honey and maple syrup.

4 Thoroughly stir the mixture.

5 Spread mixture evenly onto a lined baking tray (sheet) and bake for 15–20 minutes. During the cooking time, stir the granola a little to make sure the nuts and seeds don't burn.

Note

This lovely natural cereal is packed with energy, so only a small serve is required. It's even great without milk as a nutritious after-school snack.

creamy scrambled eggs

Serves
4
Preparation
3 mins
Cooking
8 mins
Kilojoules/Calories
1323/315
Fat
25.5g/0.9oz

Eggs are packed with protein that helps to keep you full. This tasty breakfast will stop you snacking and keep you jumping for joy all morning!

Ingredients

10 large free-range eggs
½ cup unthickened (half and half) cream
salt and freshly ground black pepper to taste
15g (0.5oz) butter
¼ cup parsley, finely chopped

1 Place the eggs, cream, salt and pepper in a bowl.

2 Gently mix until just combined. Do not over-beat or the mixture will toughen when cooked.

Equipment

3 Melt the butter in a medium frying pan (skillet) over medium heat.

4 Add the egg mixture.

5 Using a wooden spoon, very gently stir the mixture until almost cooked. Turn off heat and cover for 2 minutes. Serve on toast and top with chopped parsley.

Note
A small amount of chopped onion and grated cheese can be added to the mixture prior to cooking.

egg in a nest

Even baby birds can cook for their parents! Feed the adults in your life with these fun breakfast eggs, cooked to perfection.

Serves
4

Preparation
4 mins

Cooking
8 mins

Kilojoules/Calories
1659/395

Fat
22.6g/0.8oz

Ingredients

8 slices crusty Italian bread

2 tablespoons extra virgin olive oil

8 large free-range eggs

salt and freshly ground black pepper

1 Cut a 4cm (1.5in) hole in each of the slices of bread.

2 Brush one side of each slice of bread with olive oil.

3 Place the bread, oil-side down, in a frying pan (skillet) on medium heat.

Equipment

4 Break an egg into the hole of each slice of bread. If you need help with the pan, break the egg into a small dish first and an adult can pour the egg into the bread.

5 Once the egg starts to set, brush on a little oil and turn to cook the other side of the bread and complete the cooking of the egg.

6 Sprinkle with salt and pepper and breakfast is ready to serve.

Note

Make sure the bread is sliced thickly. To enhance the flavour, add a little butter to the pan during cooking.

smoked ham and parsley salad wraps

Serves
4
Preparation
6 mins
Kilojoules/Calories
1570.8/374
Fat
9g/0.3oz

Leave behind your ordinary sandwich and prepare to meet the super sandwich! These wraps look great and contain a huge amount of healthy food to fill you up.

Ingredients

1½ cups parsley, finely chopped

2 tomatoes, finely diced

1 large red onion, finely diced

3 teaspoons extra virgin olive oil

2 teaspoons balsamic vinegar

4 Lebanese flatbread wraps

2 tablespoons hummus

200g (7oz) lean smoked ham

80g (3oz) green salad mix

salt and pepper to taste

1 Combine the parsley, tomatoes, onion, extra virgin olive oil and balsamic vinegar in a bowl and stir gently to mix the ingredients well.

2 Spread each wrap with a little hummus.

Equipment

3 Top with the slices of smoked ham.

4 Divide the parsley salad between the wraps.

5 Add green salad mix.

6 Add salt and pepper to taste, then roll the wrap to enclose the filling.

Note

Red wine vinegar can be used to replace the balsamic vinegar. Pastrami or mortadella can replace the smoked ham.

cheesy meatballs

Makes	**20**
Preparation	**10 mins**
Cooking	**20 mins**
Kilojoules/Calories	**323.4/77**
Fat	**3g/0.1oz**

These mini meatballs are fantastic fun to make. Get your hands sticky without getting into trouble! Remember to clean up when you're finished though.

Ingredients

1 carrot
2 sticks (ribs) celery
4 mushrooms
½ cup fresh parsley
1 onion
500g (1lb) lean beef mince (ground beef)
2 eggs
40g (1.5oz) cheddar cheese (Jack cheddar), grated
1½ cups fresh wholemeal (whole wheat) breadcrumbs
½ teaspoon fresh thyme leaves, chopped
½ teaspoon fresh oregano leaves, chopped
salt and pepper to taste
400g (14oz) can chopped tomatoes

1 Preheat the oven to 200°C (400°F). Place the carrot, celery, mushrooms, parsley and onion into a food processor. Finely process the vegetables.

2 Combine the processed vegetables with beef mince (ground beef), eggs, grated cheese, breadcrumbs, thyme, oregano, and salt and pepper in a large bowl.

Equipment

3 Don't be afraid to use your hands!

4 Form into meatballs the size of a walnut.

5 Heat a non-stick frying pan (skillet) over a medium heat. Dry-fry the meatballs for 5 minutes until brown.

Note

A small quantity of leftover roasted or steamed vegetables can be puréed and included in the meatball mixture for increased nutritional value.

6 Place in a casserole dish and pour the tomatoes over the top, then cover and bake for 15 minutes. Serve with mashed potato, pasta or rice.

homemade burgers

Serves
4

Preparation
15 mins

Cooking
8 mins

Kilojoules/Calories
1554/370

Fat
11g/0.4oz

Don't let anyone call these burgers junk food: they are made with top-quality meat and even provide some of your daily greens.

Ingredients

500g (1lb) very lean beef mince (ground beef)

1 large onion, finely chopped

2 teaspoons dried oregano leaves

salt and pepper to taste

4 flat hamburger buns, split in half lengthwise

100g (3.5oz) iceberg lettuce, shredded

tomato sauce (ketchup) or barbecue sauce

3 firm tomatoes, sliced

1 Form the beef mince (ground beef) into 4 patties.

2 Place 4 patties in a large non-stick frying pan (skillet) over a medium heat.

Equipment

3 Top with a little onion, oregano leaves and salt and pepper to taste, and press onto the burger. Cook the burgers for 2–3 minutes on each side.

4 Toast the buns, then place lettuce, beef patty, sauce (ketchup) and tomato onto one half of a toasted bun.

5 Top with the other half, and serve immediately.

Note

The patties will not fall apart, even though there is no egg in the beef mince – the very lean mince and the high cooking temperature will keep the burgers together and give a lovely chargrilled flavour.

mexican roll-ups

Serves
4
Preparation
15 mins
Cooking
20 mins
Kilojoules/Calories
1377.6/328
Fat
17g/0.6oz

This combination of chicken and salsa is dreamy, and wrapping it up in tortillas (pronounced tor-TEE-yahs) topped with cheese finishes it off perfectly.

Ingredients

- 2 cups cooked chicken
- 2 tablespoons light sour cream
- 1 cup button mushrooms, finely chopped
- 300g (10oz) mild chunky tomato salsa
- 4 tortillas
- 60g (2oz) cheddar cheese (Jack cheddar), grated

1 Preheat the oven to 200°C (400°F), and grease a shallow ovenproof dish.

2 Combine the chicken, sour cream, the mushrooms and half the salsa.

Equipment

3 Divide the mixture between the 4 tortillas and roll up to enclose the filling.

4 Place tortilla parcels seam-side down in the ovenproof dish.

5 Spoon the remaining salsa over the tortillas, and finally add the grated cheese. Bake for 15–20 minutes or until the cheese turns golden.

Note

Finely chopped leftover roast vegetables, lamb, beef or pork are great in this recipe.

mini penne with chicken, cheese and tomato sauce

Serves
4
Preparation
10 mins
Cooking
10 mins
Kilojoules/Calories
2268/540
Fat
33g/1.16oz

These little pasta pots may be small, but they're packed with protein, carbs, dairy and vitamins, so they're fully rounded meals.

Ingredients

1½ cups cooked chicken breast fillet, chopped

1½ cups tomato pasta sauce

3 cups cooked mini penne or small pasta shapes

salt and pepper to taste

80g (3oz) cheddar cheese (Jack cheddar), grated

Equipment

1 Preheat the oven to 180°C (350°F) and grease 4 ramekins.

2 Combine the pasta sauce and penne.

3 Stir in the chicken.

4 Add salt and pepper to taste.

5 Divide between 4 ramekins.

6 Top with a little grated cheese and bake for 10 minutes or until cheese is golden.

Note

This recipe also works well with drained, canned tuna or cooked and chopped chicken sausages.

easy bacon pizza

Makes
24 wedges
Preparation
10 mins
Cooking
10 mins
Kilojoules / Calories
466.2/111
Fat
7g/0.24oz

Making your own pizza is the best fun – it's just so hard to decide which tasty toppings you want today!

Ingredients

2 cloves garlic, crushed

1 red capsicum (pepper), finely sliced

1 large onion, finely sliced

200g (7oz) button mushrooms, sliced

½ cup extra virgin olive oil

100g (3.5oz) bacon, chopped

½ teaspoon chilli flakes

½ cup fresh basil, chopped

1 large tomato, finely diced

6 small Lebanese flatbreads

50g (1.8oz) Parmesan cheese, grated

100g (3.5oz) cheddar cheese (Jack cheddar), grated

sprinkle of fresh oregano leaves

salt and pepper to taste

1 Preheat the oven to 200°C (400°F). Combine the garlic, capsicum (pepper), onion, mushrooms, olive oil, bacon, chilli flakes, basil and tomato in a large bowl. Cover the container and refrigerate for 10 minutes to marinate the vegetables.

2 Spray or lightly brush a little olive oil onto each Lebanese bread base.

Equipment

Note
You could add other ingredients to the basic vegetable mixture: cooked prawns (shrimp), ham, salami (pepperoni), anchovies, olives, pineapple or any of your favourite pizza toppings. To achieve the best results, add the extra toppings after first marinating the vegetables.

3 Top with marinated vegetables.

4 Sprinkle with the combined cheeses and oregano leaves. Add salt and pepper to taste. Bake on a greased baking tray (sheet) for 8–10 minutes, then serve hot from the oven. Cut each pizza into four wedges to make eating even easier.

cheese-topped ravioli

Serves
4

Preparation
5 mins

Cooking
20 mins

Kilojoules/Calories
1667.4/397

Fat
27.3g/0.96oz

The name of this pasta dish means 'wrapped up' in Italian as each is a perfect parcel of meat treats.

Ingredients

500g (1lb) beef ravioli

1½ cups pasta sauce

4 tomatoes, sliced

50g (1.8oz) Parmesan cheese, grated

50g (1.8oz) cheddar cheese (Jack cheddar), grated

1 teaspoon dried oregano leaves

½ cup dried breadcrumbs

salt and pepper to taste

1 Preheat the oven to 200°C (400°F). Cook the ravioli according to the directions on the packet.

2 Drain pasta well and place into a lasagne dish.

Equipment

3 Top with pasta sauce and sliced tomato.

4 Combine the two lots of cheese, the oregano leaves and breadcrumbs, then add salt and pepper to taste.

5 Sprinkle the cheese mixture over the tomatoes and bake for 15–20 minutes. Serve with a simple rocket (arugula) and lemon-juice salad.

Note
Leftover bolognaise sauce can be used instead of the pasta sauce for a very tasty alternative.

crispy zucchini (courgette) slices

Makes
24 slices
Preparation
6 mins
Cooking
8 mins
Kilojoules/Calories
516.6/123
Fat
7g/0.24oz

Zucchini, or courgette, is a tasty type of squash that is packed with vitamin C and other nutrients. It fills you up in no time, too!

Ingredients

- 3 large zucchini (courgette)
- 1 cup plain (all-purpose) flour
- 2 eggs, beaten with ¼ cup milk
- 2 cups fine dry breadcrumbs
- 50g (1.8oz) Parmesan cheese, grated
- 1 teaspoon dried thyme leaves
- freshly ground black pepper to taste
- ½ cup olive oil
- sweet chilli sauce, to serve
- light sour cream, to serve

1 Slice the zucchini (courgette) into thick slices on the diagonal.

2 Toss slices in flour.

Equipment

3 Coat with the egg mixture.

4 Lastly, coat well with the combined breadcrumbs, Parmesan cheese, thyme leaves and ground black pepper.

5 Fry zucchini in olive oil over medium heat until golden on each side. Serve with the sweet chilli sauce and light sour cream.

Note

Do not overcook the zucchini slices, as they won't hold their shape and will become difficult to dip in the cream and sauce.

fish bites

Try to include fish in your diet at least twice a week. It's a yummy source of protein and good fats to keep you ship-shape!

Makes
10
Preparation
6 mins
Cooking
8 mins
Kilojoules/Calories
653/156
Fat
7g/0.24oz

Ingredients

500g (1lb) firm white boneless fish, cut into ten 3cm (1.2in) cubes

½ cup plain (all-purpose) flour

2 eggs, beaten with a little milk

1 cup fine dry breadcrumbs

1 teaspoon lemon pepper seasoning

¾ cup olive oil

lemon, to serve, cut into wedges

Equipment

1 Place fish cubes into a large ziplock plastic bag with the flour. Gently shake to coat each piece of fish.

2 Dip fish into the egg mixture.

3 Then dip fish into the combined breadcrumbs and lemon pepper seasoning.

4 Fry crumbed fish pieces in olive oil on medium heat for 3–4 minutes until golden, turning a couple of times. Serve with wedges of lemon.

Note

Always remember to undercook rather than overcook your fish, to keep the texture firm and the flesh moist and delicious.

traditional
sausage rolls

Makes
36

Preparation
15 mins

Cooking
15 mins

Kilojoules/Calories
491.4/117

Fat
8g/0.28oz

Once you've tried your own homemade sausage rolls, you won't ever want to buy one from a shop again.

Ingredients

500g (1lb) sausage meat (bulk sausage)

200g (7oz) bacon, chopped

1 egg

1 teaspoon dried mixed herbs

1 teaspoon fresh oregano leaves, chopped

1 onion, very finely chopped

1 teaspoon salt

½ teaspoon ground black pepper

4 sheets premade puff pastry

milk, to glaze

1 Preheat the oven to 200°C (400°F). Thoroughly mix the sausage meat (bulk sausage), bacon, egg, mixed herbs, oregano leaves, onion, salt and pepper together in a large bowl.

2 Cut each sheet of pastry into 3 equal strips.

Equipment

3 Place a small amount of the mixture down the centre of each pastry strip.

4 Fold the pastry over to enclose the filling, then cut each of the 12 filled strips into 3 equal pieces to create 36 sausage rolls. (If you want to save some for later, you can freeze them at this point.)

5 Place the sausage roll, seam-side down, onto a baking tray (sheet) lined with baking paper, glaze with milk and bake for 15 minutes. Bake a little longer if frozen.

Note
Grated zucchini (courgette) and carrot plus finely chopped parsley may be added for extra flavour, texture and nutritional value.

apple muffins

Makes
12
Preparation
5 mins
Cooking
15 mins
Kilojoules/Calories
919.8/219
Fat
10.3g/0.36oz

Make sure you use a mini-muffin tray and these delicious treats will be just the right size to satisfy your sweet tooth.

Ingredients

2 large eggs
¾ cup milk
4 tablespoons sugar
125g (4.5oz) butter, melted
2 cups plain (all-purpose) flour
1 tablespoon baking powder
1 large Granny Smith apple, peeled and grated
  2 tablespoons icing sugar, for dusting

1 Preheat the oven to 180°C (350°F). Grease a 12-muffin mini-muffin tray.

Equipment

2 Beat the eggs, milk and sugar together in a mixing bowl.

3 Add the butter and mix well.

4 Sift the flour and baking powder, then add to the bowl.

5 Gently fold the flour into the wet ingredients.

6 Stir through the grated apple, being sure not to over-mix!

7 Place dessertspoons of the mixture into the muffin tray and bake for 12–15 minutes. Cool and dust with the icing sugar.

Note
If you're serving the muffins warm, they can be brushed with melted butter and sprinkled with cinnamon sugar.

chocolate cookies

Makes
12
Preparation
5 mins
Cooking
20 mins
Kilojoules/Calories
634.2/151
Fat
4g/0.14oz

Homemade cookies make a great present. Wrap them in parchment or waxed paper and give them in a gift bag or a pretty box.

Ingredients

2 large eggs
2 tablespoons butter, melted
¼ cup cocoa powder
1 cup sugar
pinch of salt
1 cup plain (all-purpose) flour, sifted
1 teaspoon baking powder

1 Preheat the oven to 180°C (350°F). Line a baking tray (sheet) with baking paper.

2 Break the eggs into a bowl.

Equipment

3 Add the melted butter, cocoa, sugar and salt, and combine. Then add the sifted flour and the baking powder.

4 Stir well. Make sure all the ingredients are mixed together – sometimes dry ingredients such as flour like to hide at the bottom of the bowl!

5 Place 12 spoonfuls of mixture onto the baking tray. Bake for 15–20 minutes.

Note

Include cookies as a special treat in school lunches, or serve as a sweet after-school snack.

fruity pan scones (biscuits)

Serves
6

Preparation
5 mins

Cooking
17 mins

Kilojoules/Calories
1747.2/416

Fat
5.4g/0.19oz

Treat the grown-ups in your life to some of your special scones, served with a hot drink in their favourite mug.

Ingredients

1 cup sultanas (golden raisins)

3 cups self-raising flour, sifted

1 cup milk

1 cup thickened (whipping) cream

a little extra flour

jam (jelly), to serve

extra thickened (whipping) cream, to serve

1 Add the sultanas (golden raisins) to the flour. Then add the milk and cream.

2 Using a blunt knife, stir to make a sticky dough.

Equipment

3 Turn the mixture out onto a floured board and sprinkle with a little extra flour.

4 Pat into a rectangular shape, approximately 3cm (1.2in) high.

5 Cut out scones (biscuits) with a scone (biscuit) cutter.

Note
By using an electric frying pan to cook these scones you avoid having to use your oven. A frying pan is far more economical, and means fruity pan scones are ideal for camping!

6 Place scones in an electric frying pan (skillet) lined with baking paper. Cook, covered, on medium for 5 minutes. Turn scones and cook for a further 5–8 minutes. Alternatively, the scones can be cooked in a conventional oven, preheated to 220°C (430°F), for 15 minutes. Serve 2 per person with jam (jelly) and cream.

chocky road cupcakes

Makes
12

Preparation
12 mins

Cooking
20 mins

Kilojoules/Calories
2958.1/707

Fat
50g/1.76oz

These cupcakes have a long list of ingredients but are surprisingly quick and easy to make – and definitely worth it!

Ingredients

3 eggs
½ cup butter, softened
1 cup castor (berry) sugar
½ cup milk
1½ cups self-raising flour, sifted
1 teaspoon vanilla essence
1 tablespoon cocoa powder

Topping

½ cup milk chocolate bits
½ cup butter, softened
⅓ cup thickened (whipping) cream
1½ cups icing sugar
1 teaspoon vanilla essence
¼ cup glacé (glazed) cherries, chopped
⅓ cup almonds, chopped
⅓ cup marshmallows, chopped

1 Preheat the oven to 160°C (320°F). Line a 12-cupcake pan with cupcake papers.

2 In a medium-sized bowl, lightly beat the eggs, then add butter and sugar.

Equipment

3 Mix until light and fluffy.

4 Add milk, flour, vanilla essence and cocoa powder.

5 Stir to combine. Then beat with an electric mixer for 2 minutes, until light and creamy.

Topping

1 While the cupcakes are in the oven, you can make the topping. Combine the chocolate bits and half of the butter in a medium-sized saucepan over a medium heat. As the mixture begins to melt, reduce heat to low, stirring constantly, until melted. Remove from heat, add cream, and stir. Rest for 10 minutes: the mixture will be firm and velvety in consistency.

2 Combine remaining butter, icing sugar and vanilla essence, and stir until light and fluffy. Add melted chocolate mixture and stir to combine.

3 Ice the top of each cupcake and decorate with pieces of cherry, almond and marshmallow.

6 Divide the mixture evenly between the cupcake papers. Bake for 18–20 minutes until risen and firm to touch. Cool for a few minutes and then transfer to a wire rack. Cool fully before icing.

banana pancakes

Makes
6–8

Preparation
5 mins

Cooking
6 mins

Kilojoules/Calories
1079.4/257

Fat
9.2g/0.32oz

This delicious dessert is a classic combination of pancake and toppings with an extra serving of fruit. It's a win-win situation!

Ingredients

- 2 cups pancake mix or 375g (13.5oz) shaker pack
- 2 medium bananas, sliced
- 2 tablespoons butter
- ¼ cup cinnamon sugar
- 1⅓ cups golden (corn) syrup
- 6 small scoops ice-cream

1 Following the instructions on the pack, make up the pancake batter. Combine the batter and sliced banana.

2 Heat small dollops of the butter in a frying pan (skillet) on low heat.

Equipment

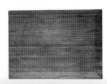

3 Drop large spoonfuls of mixture into the butter in the pan.

4 Cook until bubbles appear on the surface. Turn and cook until golden in colour.

5 Serve with a good sprinkle of cinnamon sugar, syrup and a scoop of ice-cream.

Note

Your family members might have their own favourite pancake topping that you can try: fresh lemon juice, cream, maple syrup, jam (jelly) or even custard!

fabulous fruit salad

Serves
4
Preparation
5 mins
Kilojoules/Calories
330/78.6
Fat
0.1g/0.005oz

This is one of the healthiest ways to end your meal. It's low in fat and provides much of the fruit goodness you need in a day.

Ingredients

1 peach
1 green apple
1 red apple
1 mango
a few slices cantaloupe (rockmelon)
1 punnet (packet) strawberries
generous sprinkle of mint flakes
375g (13oz) canned pineapple pieces (tidbits) with juice
sugar to taste

1 Dice all the fruit ingredients except the pineapple.

2 Gently mix together in a bowl.

Equipment

3 Add the mint flakes and the pineapple pieces (tidbits) with juice.

4 Gently stir through.

5 This fabulous fruit should be nice and sweet. If you want an extra treat, dust the fruit salad lightly with sugar. Refrigerate until cool.

honeydew heaven

Honeydew melon contains fruity goodness but tastes super-sweet!

Serves
2

Preparation
5 mins

Kilojoules/Calories
230/55

Fat
0.2g/0.007oz

Ingredients

½ cup diced honeydew
1 teaspoon lime juice
1 tablespoon white sugar
6 ice cubes
1 large slice of cantaloupe (rockmelon)
½ cup lime-flavoured drink

1 Place all ingredients except lime-flavoured drink and cantaloupe (rockmelon) in blender; blend until smooth.

2 Divide mixture between 2 glasses.

Equipment

3 Scoop out 3 to 4 balls of cantaloupe flesh, and place in glasses.

4 Top up with lime-flavoured drink and give a gentle stir.

strawberry smoothie

Serves
2
Preparation
5 mins
Kilojoules/Calories
887/212
Fat
9g/0.31oz

Six strawberries provide a good dose of vitamin C and can whiten your teeth, too.

Ingredients

½ cup milk
6 frozen strawberries
½ cup plain yoghurt
1 teaspoon honey
2–3 drops vanilla essence
pinch of nutmeg (optional)
4 ice cubes
extra strawberry to garnish

1 Place all ingredients except garnish in blender; blend until smooth.

2 Pour into chilled glasses.

Equipment

3 Serve topped with half a fresh strawberry.

banana smoothie

This sweet, thick drink is comforting whatever the weather is like.

Serves
2
Preparation
5 mins
Kilojoules/Calories
887/212
Fat
9g/0.31oz

Ingredients

½ cup milk
1½ bananas
½ cup plain yoghurt
1 teaspoon honey
2–3 drops vanilla essence
4 ice cubes
sprinkle of nutmeg
(optional)

1 Place all ingredients except nutmeg in blender; blend until smooth.

2 Pour into chilled glasses.

Equipment

3 Serve topped with a sprinkle of nutmeg.

strawberry swirl

Try this frozen fruity drink when you need to be refreshed.

Serves
2
Preparation
5 mins
Kilojoules/Calories
213/51
Fat
2g/0.07oz

Ingredients

4 frozen strawberries
dash of cinnamon
1 ice cube
1 cup milk
4 tablespoons strawberry topping

Equipment

1 Put all ingredients except the milk and 2 tablespoons of strawberry topping into a blender and blend until an icy puree is formed. Place the puree in a small bowl and put the bowl into the freezer.

2 Don't rinse the blender! While the bowl is in the freezer, add 1 cup of milk and 2 tablespoons of strawberry topping to blender and blend until frothy.

3 Spoon half the frozen pulp into the bottom of each glass and drizzle a dash of topping around the sides.

4 Top up with strawberry milkshake and serve.

index